MW01016129

ALSO BY TIMOTHY TAYLOR

The Blue Light Project
Silent Cruise
Story House
Stanley Park
The Cranky Connoisseur

www.timothytaylor.ca

*For Richard
with best wishes.*

FOODVILLE

Biting Dispatches
from a Food-obsessed City

Timothy Taylor

N

www.nonvella.com

Library and Archives Canada
Cataloguing in Publication

Taylor, Timothy L., 1963-, author

Foodville: biting dispatches from a well-fed
city / Timothy Taylor.

Issued in print and electronic formats.
ISBN 978-0-9936216-2-8 (pbk.)
ISBN 978-0-9936216-5-9 (ebook)

1. Food habits. 2. Food in popular culture.
3. Food—Social aspects. I. Title.

TX357.T39 2014   641.3   C2014-904344-9
                                C2014-904345-7

1

---//---

NOT VERY MANY people will immediately remember Mike Kalina's name, though his story is quintessentially of his era. Kalina was the *Pittsburgh Post-Gazette* food critic in the late eighties and early nineties, writing under the name "The Travelin' Gourmet," which was also the name of his television show and his 1990 cookbook. The book is now out of print, but you can still find copies online for as little as 99 cents. It has recipes for things like Chicken Wings in Oyster Sauce, Crab Cheesecake, and something called Enraged Spaghetti, which was Kalina's novelty name for *spaghetti aglio e olio*—pasta with garlic, hot pepper flakes and olive oil—a preparation for which you can now obtain 145,000 more-or-less-identical recipes in just 0.29 seconds via Google.

Every city in the West at that time had a Kalina. These were the reviewers and cookbook writers whose tastes and dishes reflected the culinary zeitgeist of the day, a time that I now think of as the Great Era of Culinary Evangelism in North America. We were all suddenly hearing about how we could have a new relationship with food: close and personal and full of hitherto unavailable expertise. We could all be *connoisseurs*.

And there were highlights and lowlights in the first generation of food celebrities who were then created. There were Jacques Pépin, Julia Child and James Barber on the one hand. But then, we also had the reinvented Graham Kerr in his yuppie braces with his white board and calorie calculations. There was the shrieking Jeff Smith, the Frugal Gourmet soon to be disgraced. I could go on. But the point is that these evangelists—the skillful and the schlocky alike—were serving to awaken what would become the most important new market phenomenon of the late twentieth and early twenty-first centuries: the consumer foodie.

Kalina's photo on his cookbook gives emblem to this emerging enthusiasm. There were dozens of cookbooks from the era with almost identical covers: the author standing behind a cutting board stacked artfully with kitchen gear and ingredients. Apples, some pastry mid-prep, copper pots and a rolling pin. And always a very particular facial expression: a commingling of astonishment, delight and encouragement. Hey, the author-cook seems invariably to be saying, you can do this too! So Kalina, on the cover of The Travelin' Gourmet, stands with his hands spread and a look of beatific joy across chefly-florid features.

All the more shocking, then, that Kalina killed himself just two years after the photo was taken, in January 1992. Chefs, we understand from obscurely sad news items over the years, do occasionally suicide under the tremendous pressures of their trade. Bernard Loiseau, Jérôme Girardot, Brian Drysdale come to mind. Italian television chef Antonio Carluccio would be on the list, too, but he merely collapsed a lung when he stabbed himself in the chest with a pair of kitchen scissors.

But food critics? Whoever heard of a critic killing himself? And while the truth about Kalina will never be known, a February 1992 piece that ran in the New York Times after his death suggests that professional pressures may have contributed to his tragic decision. The piece says: "...what friends say might have undone Mr. Kalina was finding out in late January that the Postal Service and US Attorney in Pittsburgh were investigating his financial dealings with restaurants." Among the allegations, the Times reported, were statements to the effect that Kalina and a partner had received payments from restaurant owners in exchange for positive reviews.

We can't know now the full motives for the investigation, or if indeed it involved actual wrong-doings at all. But what struck me on first reading the story, and has been on my mind again more recently, is that even the casting of aspersion on the reputation of a food critic – at that time, just over 20 years ago – might have generated such devastating fall-out.

Maybe I'm moved by the tragedy in part because I've recently become a food writer myself. But I think the bigger reason has to do with the cultural sea change implied. That change was first suggested to me by a friend over lunch at Fuel Restaurant on West Fourth Avenue in Kitsilano in Vancouver, where we both live. In the few years since, that popular restaurant has morphed twice, first to Re-Fuel and then to Fable, a farm-to-table operation (the name for which emerged from chef Trevor Bird's participation in the television show *Top Chef*). But back when it was Fuel (I think it was a shoe store before that) the two of us sat and discussed Kalina, feeling genuinely perplexed and saddened. My friend, a retired philosophy professor, had specialized in the writings of Jean-Jacques Rousseau and Bernard Mandeville during his career, studying the Enlightenment-era voices that articulate with greatest clarity the seminal arguments about consumer culture in the West. (They called this The Luxury Debate, back then. Mandeville was pro, Rousseau con, roughly.) And I remember at some point in our discussion my friend putting his fork down next to his ploughman's lunch, the hand-crafted fixings of which—salami, rillettes, gherkins, et cetera—would have been so alien to the hippy Kitsilano of 1968 that first drew him to Vancouver that they might have originated on another planet. And here he shook his head, finally giving voice to the brutal irony of the suicide.

"But today," he said, "even if a food critic were paid by restaurants for their reviews, and it was proven, it wouldn't make any difference, would it?"

And he's right. What might have been considered an ethical breach back then (if payment for reviews had ever been established) is routine now in the era of crowd-sourced criticism, where a recent study estimates that as many as 15 percent of social media restaurant reviews—those appearing on popular sites like Yelp, Urbanspoon and Tripadvisor—are paid for by restaurant owners. But only 20 years ago, so great was the potential breach of faith that a man might feel pressed toward such a brink.

Which is why Mike Kalina should be remembered, especially by foodies. And not just in Pittsburgh or Vancouver, which like so many cities today cherishes the legend of its own culinary prowess. Talking food is talking about ourselves: our restaurants, our food trucks, our celebrities, our number of features on Diners, Drive-ins and Dives. We should remember Kalina because he came before all that. From a time when we still assumed the critic to be outside of the phenomenon described, a time before food passed beyond objectivity and subjectivity entirely, and moved over into the wholly mimetic realm: that mirrored funhouse hall of fashion.

2

————— // —————

I F YOU'VE BEEN following food in your city for the past decade or more, take a test. Which of these statements by your own local food critics were published in that time? These are Vancouver-specific examples, but swap the city name and they could have come from anywhere.

"Vancouver eating has never been better."

"Never have we eaten so well, and never has our knowledge of what we eat been so great."

"Vancouver has emerged as one of the leading culinary laboratories on earth."

"These days, it seems Vancouver is the It Girl of global food cities."

"The story of British Columbia's climb to culinary stardom is written in the constellations... "

"Vancouver food critics all seem to have drunk deeply of the purple Kool-Aid."

That last one is mine, and I am being facetious. But the quotes preceding it, and many, many similar examples, have appeared steadily over the course of the past fifteen years. The issue isn't whether the critics are right or wrong. The issue is that this lock-step enthusiasm signaled something over time, revealing that the root motivation of critique was not the desire to submit the cultural phenomenon of food to real analysis: Is this plate good? Is it good compared to that plate? Is this whole connoisseurship project worth the effort?

Instead, these reviews, and millions of words worth of other food writing at the time, were born of the desire to advertise one's affiliation with the next new thing. And nobody then or now need feel any shame knowing that fact, and certainly nobody needs to feel *suicidal*. Because all of us—the writers and readers, the diners and the restaurants, the "elite" Yelpers and "prime" Urbanspooners—we've all been in on it.

3

----//----

FOOD, FOOD. YOU have to step back and ask: How and why did we all get so hepped up about food? When I flash back on my childhood cuisine—and I mean *flash*, just grabbing the first image of food my memory will serve—I get a Safeway bag of frozen mixed vegetables. Diced carrots with peas and corn kernels that you boiled, and when you bit into them you got the flavor of poached cardboard. That was food to me and I was more or less unaware of any alternatives. Or, that's not quite true. I was aware that my mother could knock out stellar north European dishes, mingled unusually with flavors and dishes of South America, where she and my father met and lived for many years: spaetzle, rouladen, ceviche, *arroz con pollo*. But I was equally aware that she rarely had the time to do so. So you made do with the poached cardboard.

We've all changed. You have. I have. We've come so far around the corner on food options and food expertise and our willingness to invest time and money and effort on food that we now have a chorus of critics saying we've gone too far.

Alison Pearlman's 2013 book, *Smart Casual: The Transformation of Gourmet Restaurant Style in America*, comprehensively dismantles the myths of foodie-ism: the false-democratization of comfort food, the "ingredient fascism" of your average urban locavore with their one-percenter food budgets. B.R. Myers went even further in his 2011 screed in the *Atlantic*, "The Moral Crusade Against Foodies," advancing a case that might be interpreted to mean we were all somehow *better people* when we ate those bags of frozen mixed vegetables.

Of course, at this moment in history, their criticism merely highlights the intensity of food enthusiasm in virtually every other cultural quarter. True story: I was at a literary festival. My first novel, *Stanley Park*, had just been published, a book about the trials of a young chef. After the reading I was answering some questions and a woman asked me—tentatively, exploring the possibilities of the word—"Are you a... *foodie?*"

Maybe I could have given a more nuanced answer. I pay attention to what I eat. I cook every day. I'm good at it. Did I ever build a holiday around finding *poulet Bresse* and *crottin de Chavignol?* Yes. Yes, I did that once. And still, even from up front, on the stage, I could hear a warble in the question, a quiver of self-doubt, or need. And I found myself wishing suddenly not to contribute to it. So I blurted out: "I am not now, nor have I ever been, a *foodie.*"

Big laughs. But laughs that tapered quickly. Surprised laughs. Slightly deflated laughs. I knew what was going on the instant I make the joke. There wasn't a person in the room, of several hundred people, who *didn't* self-identify as a foodie. I may not have offended anybody, but I had no doubt confused them.

Sure enough, a man came up to me at the book-signing table an hour later. I could see what was coming before he said a word. The sentiment was etched on his brow, in the troubled creases around his mouth. He said to me, "You know, I just have to say how very disappointed my wife and I were to hear you say that you're not a foodie."

He still bought a book, and he still wanted it signed. I was tempted to write: *I'm sorry*. But there's no being sorry for these things. Food was a tribe that had newly formed. In it, people were finding some kind of intense comfort they'd been missing elsewhere. Who was I not to join?

4

——————//——————

I WAS RAISED IN Vancouver, but moved away with my family when I was in my teens. I came back pretty much as soon as I could, about a decade later. I was married and in my first job (banking, to which, it would soon dawn on me, I was entirely unsuited). This was 1987. My wife and I moved into an apartment the city's West End just off storied Davie Street, with its mingling of gay clubs, sex shops, breakfast joints and at least one very fine French patisserie. We had a narrow galley kitchen with glass-front cabinets and a creaky old gas range. I had two cookbooks, which I'd worked my way through, front to back. *La Technique* and *La Methode*, both by master French chef Jacques Pépin. Salmon with beurre blanc. Stuffed squid stewed in tomatoes. *Poulet a la crapaudine*. (*Crapaudine* is not a particularly nice word, is it? But then, they say spatchcocked in English, which is worse.)

So I cooked and cooked, up and down the Pépin repertoire.

And when we weren't doing that, we hung out at La Bodega, which was our "third space" before Starbucks colonized and then later abandoned the term. A rotating crew of a dozen of us would gather there, and I still remember the menu almost verbatim. *Patatas bravas,* chorizo. Chicken livers, calamari, ceviche, *ensalada Bodega* (which was like church-picnic potato salad with peas and bits of shrimp and red pepper in it). *Anticuchos* meat skewers and *morcilla* blood sausage. (These last two were always written on the chalkboard up front, never on the paper menu.) And sangria, of course, the "secret" ingredient of which was Coke. The only thing nobody ever ordered off that menu, as I recall, was the *empanada,* described as "a delightful little pie" on the menu. Although we also never failed to read it aloud from the menu, as if we might order it.

"How about a delightful little pie?" someone would ask. Nobody would ever answer.

La Bodega, in the end, was a victim of its own success, which is what happens to things that find themselves adrift on fashion's sea. Discovery, popularity, inevitable decline. That is the mimetic spiral of fashion, having nothing to do with objective value or subjective experience, and everything to do with perceived esteem. Fashion lives in the eye of the observer and, as Rousseau lamented, those beholden to fashion must therefore look to the observer to find the very sentiment of their own existence, which is to say, the validation of their own public worth.

Of course, La Bodega was only one example of the broader phenomenon going on in Vancouver then, that monumental phase change of the ascendance of food. But at La Bodega it meant lineups stretching out the front door. It meant that the coveted front table under the bull's head became impossible to get. And it meant the appeal of La Bodega gradually became diluted, the esteem value of each experience there beginning to plummet.

And all that would have been bad enough without me trying to write a story about the scene, at the very apogee of the craze, like an elegy. A poetic fiction set at a restaurant called The Cosmo, where a gang of late twenty-somethings gathered and ate tapas and drank sangria and talked about hating their jobs, or being broke, or the films of Errol Morris.

I cringe, thinking about that now. The Cosmo story was far too "sticky," as John Updike once said about everything Scott Fitzgerald wrote other than *The Great Gatsby*. Which is to say, far too embarrassingly transparent on the topic of what the author wished the world to think of them. My story strained to evoke an author who was that archetypical person who had so recently become magnetic to status: tapas-literate, secret-ingredient knowing, front-table sitting, film-discussing, all-round-cultured, plugged-in, food-savvy dude.

The world was turning, fast. Mike Kalina was dead in his car in Pittsburgh, asphyxiated by carbon monoxide. The era of Fashion Food was on us, and nothing was ever going to be the same.

EVERY CITY PRODUCED its own homegrown culinary evangelists during this period, amateurs with passion who were spreading the good word. Julia Child was perhaps the senior, global example. In the SNL skit where Dan Aykroyd parodied the

greatest amateur cook of all time, it's notable that he spoofed
her ploughing on with her prep despite having cut herself and
begun to geyser blood. The comic idea was plain enough: on one
level, the people doing this kind of thing, upgraded from frozen
vegetables to French cookery, were masochistic nutcases. Leave
it to the pros, folks. For God's sake, eat out!

Our own evangelist of the period was the aforementioned
James Barber. Originally an engineer by trade, Barber champi-
oned an assertively simple and easy-going approach to food.
"Cooking is like sex," he would say with a shrug. "You do the best
with what you have." Sausages and cabbage. Cauliflower with
cheddar cheese. Chicken breasts sautéed with cherry tomatoes and peas (frozen, the one time I saw him do it). On his
television show, he did no prep or pre-cooking before the cam-
eras rolled, once promising that he could finish a meal before
anybody watching could get a pizza delivered. He was, in this
lack of pretention, the single greatest contribution to food
that had ever came out of my city, an anti-self-aggrandizer, at
least on-camera and in his books. I think he captured his entire
culinary worldview quite perfectly in fourteen syllables when
writing on the topic of stew.

"It's simple and delicious. So quit being such a snob."

Vancouver really should have that inscribed somewhere,
prominently. Perhaps in marigolds on the embankment south
of Grant McConachie Way, for people to read as they exit the
airport and enter the city. But it won't ever get this treatment.
You know it and I know it. Because Barber, similarly to Kalina,
midwifed the arrival of the food era that would render the sentiment outdated, insufficiently refined.

I bumped into Barber and his partner at Feast of Fields once.
There were grateful crowds around the heirloom tomatoes
and people standing out in the middle of fields, having their

moments. I wrote a scene for *Stanley Park* based on that day: I had my sous-chef character, Jules, making crostini with mush-rooms, which of course I saw being made at Feast of Fields. I didn't have her making pine-needle sorbet, however, which was also being handed out.

I knew Barber's partner, though had never met the man him-self. But he was in my culinary pantheon, up there with Pépin and Child. I felt like asking him for an autograph, but was too nervous. So I tried to impress him instead, casting about for something suitable to say and coming up with *pine-needle sorbet.* "Have you tried it? You really have to."

Barber's face squinted up, a rictus of incredulity. "Pine nee-dles?" he said. "Did you say *pine needles*? I could have sworn you said pine needles."

What was I doing? I didn't even like the pine-needle sorbet. Jules would have thought the pine-needle sorbet was *silly.*

6

ACK TO THE critics. It isn't my plan to name a bunch from the past decade and heap scorn. I've met most of them and I like them. They tend to be smart people, those who manage to land one of the most coveted jobs in the world. The competition is stiff. Here's what I think, though. I think that some critics write positive reviews and others are in a state of perpetual peeve, and that it makes little difference to either restaurants or diners. Because in the end, each critic is a flavor, a dish on a menu that readers choose based on mood and taste. The critic and the diner have themselves become the subjects of contemporary food criticism. Welcome to the Food Fashion Era in Foodville.

1996. A critical year in the development of this reality. This was the year a food critic in Vancouver wrote a "review" of Diva at the Met, which was then the jewel in the city's culinary crown. I'd argue that here we have a foundational document in the evolution of culinary Vancouver and elsewhere, in that here for the first time we have a full-on revelation, by a critic, of their own helpless entanglement in the subject.

The review did not gush praise, it hemorrhaged praise. It died operatically of praise. It chose words as if to emphasize that it wasn't criticism at all, but rather a single homage designed to obviate any requirement for further discussion. *Once and for all*, the review seemed to say, *let's just have done with the sheer, untrammeled perfection of the Diva.* The bar was "glamorous." The barstools were "seductive." The staff was "the city's most stellar culinary talent." The room was—ready?—"candlelit and romantic."

When the critic started eating, however, not even praise would suffice. Ingredients prepared with "infinite care and patience" eluded the grasp of language. So we must make do with pledges on behalf of the critic's experience. "A write up of Maria Callas at her finest could probably substitute for a Diva review." And on the wine list, we are assured, "pages could be written." Here the critic fell on his/her own pen, surrendering in a crash of timpani to the incommunicable excellence to which his/her palate had been submitted.

Maybe Diva really was that good. I wish I could tell you, but I only ate there once and don't remember a thing except that it was the kind of cuisine we saw a lot of at the leading edge of the Food Fashion Era: bits of things stacked artfully, swirls of goop and lotion on a plate.

Other critics on Diva:

"Sometimes the best clings to your senses like Velcro."

"Eating his food was a revelation; seeing such grace, elegance and finesse in such a young man was humbling."

"Diva at the Met is doing a menu that has me festively anointed with drool."

Well, come on. Who's going to argue with that? The critic was *drooling*.

7

—————————— *//* ——————————

WE ALL WENT gaga for Lumière and Rob Feenie after that. Best French Restaurant in the city for a full decade running, according to *Vancouver* magazine, right up to 2005. Was it worth the fuss? The answer is subjective, of course. For many people it obviously was. Speaking personally, I ate the tasters menu once. My agent was paying. This is the kind of place you only go if your agent is paying. Forget the fact that Lumière was originally pitched as being reasonably priced. And forget anybody who ever told you Lumière was about simple French cooking.

"...the backbone of Feenie's cuisine is an emphasis on taste and simplicity..."

"...simplifying the components of each dish to their raw essence while making the total result even more complex..."

Or this one: "...simple, shining results."

Here is Feenie being simple and shining: "*ratte* potatoes and Périgord truffles with cauliflower puree, spinach, foie gras emulsion and red wine beef jus."

Foie-gras emulsion, folks. Of course, this up-talking the simplicity of Lumière was going on from the very beginning. Back in the mid-nineties, a reviewer inadvertently wrote something funny about Lumière. "Why is it difficult to get a really good bowl of pasta in Vancouver at a reasonable price? Many suffer the pizza topping syndrome of too many ingredients. More is not merrier when it comes to noodles."

A couple of blocks down the street from Tang's Noodle House, which at the time was one of James Barber's picks, the reviewer's long quest for simple noodles was at last over at... Lumière. Here it comes: pappardelle tossed with shredded duck confit, roasted garlic, tomatoes and basil.

Shredded duck confit? Delicious, no doubt. But was its application to a bowl of pappardelle the solution to an established simple-pasta deficit in Vancouver in the mid-nineties? No it emphatically was not. So why say something is simple when it clearly isn't simple? Why the tout-worthiness of the word simple? Who said simple was necessarily good in the first place? Well, Rob Feenie did. And Feenie's face was on the back of buses in those days.

Jacques Lacan: *We desire the desire of the other.*

Or, as the literary theorist-philosopher-psychoanalyst might have had it in this particular case: *At that moment we desired the perceived desires of Rob Feenie, which is to say, we desired the adoration that he was then attracting.*

Of course, there came a point when that equation didn't work anymore. When Feenie disappeared from view, like magic, we all suddenly desired the desire of David Hawksworth, later Warren Geraghty, later still Robert Belcham, Lucais Syme, David Gunawan. But I'm getting ahead of myself. Back to my tasters menu.

My agent, a friend and serious gourmand, sprang for the tasters menu with flights of wine. I remember our little foie-gras aps came to the table. Yay! Foie gras! (Goops and lotions, check, check.) But then something unexpected and funny happened. I knew a waiter who worked at a restaurant next door to Lumière (a mid-market casual joint at the time). He had somehow heard that I was in Lumière, celebrating the publication of my first novel with my agent, and he sent over a drink.

He sent over a drink from one restaurant to another, which I—alone in the room—found very funny. It was funny because he carried it in through the front door and handed it to the maitre d', who had to carry this thing across the dining room, as if people were just ordering in extra booze off the street. And it was also funny because, into the *minceur* minimalism and haute-cuisinery of Lumière, my friend chose to send me a massive Cancun Spring Break-style margarita. It was in this enormous glass. It almost didn't fit on the table. Of course I remember the margarita. How am I ever going to forget it? I also remember Feenie—pink-faced, strapped into his whites— peering out the kitchen door at my margarita.

But I don't remember a thing about the foie gras. OK, maybe

one thing. I remember that, like my margarita, the sauce was green.

Mike. That was the name of the waiter I knew from the place that used to be next door to the restaurant that used to be Lumière. And if I didn't ever say it before, I really should say it now: Thank you, Mike.

8

———— // ————

WHAT DOES FASHION Food get us? Experimentation, which can be a good thing. There's that old saw about the man who ate the first oyster. Somebody has to experiment. Does it always work? Uh, no.

Dishes from the early years which I don't see coming up again any time soon:

Lobster hot pot with black beans, garlic, ginger and miso. This is what you might call gilding the lily. Assuming that tasting the lobster is part of the reason you pay for one, I wouldn't go the black bean, garlic, ginger and miso route.

Smoked foie-gras ravioli with sweet-and-sour sauce. Multilevel grotesquery, this. I am dubious about the needless smoking of the liver of a force-fed goose. I distrust the loading of it into ravioli. I am repulsed by the idea of sweet-and-sour sauce coming anywhere near anything else on the plate.

Steak in Marsala sauce with risotto al Barolo. Marsala and Barolo. I assume the vegetables that accompany this dish have been poached in Sauternes. Perhaps Asti Spumante as an accompaniment.

Smoked eel and pineapple with a red-wine sauce. Ay caramba. I couldn't make that one up. Swirling in the imitative cyclone of Vancouver fine dining, however, chef David Hawksworth was at least once up to it. And if that mouthful of eel and pineapple and red-wine reduction was in fact delicious, anyone, please contact me. But I won't hold my breath.

9

———— // ————

AFTER LUMIÈRE—IN WHAT is a critical and illuminating passage in the opening of the Food Fashion Era—for a while all critical roads in Vancouver led to the newcomer, West. It was the *ne plus ultra* for several years before the foodie gaze drifted away to rested on Campagnolo, La Quercia, Hawksworth, others.

But we can't actually get to West without first saying first saying a word about C Restaurant, which until 2013 was overseen by chef Rob Clark and which has occupied a special place at the wailing wall of Vancouver food criticism over the years. Here we've climbed out of the early, nervously effusive food enthusiasm of the nineties and into the throbbing, desiring heart of the twenty-first century's first decade in food. In the wake of 9/11, you could make a case, we all began to eat as if we really needed the distraction. But we also ate as if we were seeking a way not merely to be full, for our flavor receptors to be amused and satisfied. We began to eat as if it were an avenue toward some moral and social good. In the case of C, this played out interestingly. Critics tended to agree that the restaurant was a very fine example of very fine dining, though never quite enough to ever name it the city's best. That withholding of ultimate honors will have had any number of underlying justifications, only one of which (in my mind) is that putting gold leaf on an oyster is bullshit. There, I said it. Gold leaf on anything you eat is bullshit. And C did that (perhaps they still do). And I think we all know, in our heart of hearts, that eating gold leaf is what people do right before the end of civilization.

Which of course did not happen. Civilization survived and C thrives to this day. I had myself a couple of solid meals there, gold leaf notwithstanding. And yet, I would still beg to differ with the ecstatic tone of the C press, which has over the years seemed crafted not to praise the culinary project but the broader cultural one. Perhaps this was compensatory for the senior accolade perpetually withheld, but it nevertheless said far more about what was going on in the dining room—in that seething consumer consciousness, desiring in volatile ways—than it did about what Clark was doing in the kitchen. No, I did not then or now view C as filling "…a big void in reminding us that Vancouver is a coastal city." I am reminded of the ocean hourly in more prosaic ways, like, say, by looking at the view, smelling the sea air, et cetera. And, sorry, but I would never rate C as "…a national treasure…" either. Did C "take diners deep inside the lexicon of our local fishery"? Okay, possibly it did that. Sort of. But the day I agreed that C Restaurant was Vancouver's "social conscience" would be the day I leave this city. Our social conscience would be people trying to eliminate homelessness or find a cure for AIDS. Sustainable harvesting of our natural resources is critical, yes. And Clark was always to be commended for leaning his cuisine hard in that direction. But this kind of thing…

"Talk about leadership... C, you're a Best in the West winner in the best sense of the word. Thank you from all of us."

Good grief.

Which brings us back to West.

Feenie flamed and Lumière foundered. An unhappy story. He was the Lumière brand and the place didn't survive long even when the owners brought in international heavy Daniel Boulud to replace him. But Feenie gone was also epoch-shifting for critics and diners. At his apex he was being described as Scheherazade and Glenn Gould and Bach, all in the same review. (Why not Rimsky-Korsakov himself? Why not Mozart for that matter?) One minute he's earning spittle-spackled praise for "layering suave flavors built on contrapunts of texture." The next minute he's working for upscaled Hooters clone Cactus Club—and West is winning all the category-killing praise, first under David Hawksworth, then under Warren Geraghty.

West had taken the crown. And critics were rare who disagreed, as if the crown-passing were perhaps more important than anything that could really be said about the food at all. Certainly the place was impressive. Walking to the restrooms, you pass down a hallway hung with dozens of awards, local and international, for the wine, the service, the food. And, of course, the local press has been stellar too. Maybe not quite "written in the constellations," but not for lack of trying.

"Sophisticated, excellent, innovative and always impressive."

"...the most technically assured cooking in the city, exacting use of ingredients from the butter on the table to the tea and coffee after the meal, a comfortable room and excellent service..."

I went once with friends to see what the fuss was about. For an appetizer, my wife had pan-seared arctic char with grilled-fennel coleslaw, dill hollandaise and blood-orange dressing. I ate a terrine of smoked rabbit and lobster with a tarragon white-bean parfait. Across the table, our friends had cream of Jerusalem artichoke soup with a Dungeness crab crepe floating in it, and ravioli of calamari braised in white wine with potato-and-chorizo cassoulet and crispy calamari. I'm typing out all that to make the point that this is clearly sophisticated and technical food. It is certainly not "rigorously casual local food," as a critic wrote. Neither is it "quietly exciting." These are plates with an orchestral array of ingredients. Sitting in front of us, they reminded me of the artist Joseph Cornell's little diorama boxes, dibbed and dabbed with color and sprouting with a perplexing array of tiny bits. I found myself imagining a troop of culinary oompa-loompas at work with microscopes and tweezers. Although, watching from our table—just in front of the service window—I could see that assemblage fell to Geraghty and his sous, who hunched next to each other over each plate, faces inches from the food, piling things on with their fingers or scooping off dainty spoonfuls of this or that garnish or sauce to dollop and adorn the plates.

Artful, make no mistake. My terrine was swirled around with something emerald green. Very pretty. My wife's arctic char was balanced on the little bird's nest of slaw, tiny cubes of blood orange spilling to the plate. The Dungeness crab crepe was tied shut with a chive. Et cetera, et cetera.

The verdict on taste? All solid except for mine. That was strange. I love rabbit anything. But in order of their menu appearance, all the elements of my terrine went rather demure on my palate. I couldn't taste much smokiness, rabbit or lobster. But then, I'm not at all clear why there was lobster in a rabbit terrine in the first place. Innovative, but not excellent. Still, everyone else enjoyed theirs, so Geraghty was three for four.

Mains, however, didn't do as well. I have to drop another review quote on you, because this is more or less precisely what our dinner was not:

"A transcendent food experience... When the elements come together, my being goes 'Wow!'"

The critic's *being* went wow. Holy smokes. I would be happy to get some of that action. But I have to report that while my being remained interested, it was un-wowed.

Here were the plates: (1) veal sweetbread wrapped in smoked tongue with Nova Scotia lobster sweet-fennel purée and crispy shredded veal and bisque jus; (2) braised pork belly *au poivre* with a tournedos (singular) of Kurobuta pork, creamy polenta, citrus-glazed winter vegetables and quince purée; (3) duo of Vancouver Island venison, roasted loin and rich braised shoulder, crisp-toasted potatoes and watercress; and, finally, (4) curry-scented *ballotine* of Maple Hill chicken, cauliflower and sweet raisins, *sag aloo* ravioli.

See Joseph Cornell and oompa-loompas, above. The plates glided onto the table linen looking as if a crew with thousands of kitchen hours of experience had worked them over with micrometers and laser levels. The chicken arrived in three perfectly tubular portions, each recloaked in its skin and topped with garnish. The veal sweatbread had been wrapped in the smoked tongue and sliced. The tournedos was about the size of a golf ball and seemed to tremble in place next to a smudge of quince purée. Very sophisticated.

But flavor? The tiny coil of pork belly on my plate was tasty, but the rest was a bit pale. The sweetbreads scored, but the smoked tongue was overcooked and dry. The crispy veal garnish was crisp to the point that its only flavor was *crispness*. It could have been filaments of pork rind. My friend who ordered the venison said he wished he'd ordered the calamari ravioli appetizer again as a main course. And the chicken order fared even worse.

"The roast chicken you made us the other night?" my friend said. "Way better." And that was a Maple Hills bird too. Salt and pepper. 425 degrees for about 70, 75 minutes. A splash of white wine into the pan to make some sauce.

So, West. A transcendent experience? I just can't agree and we ate almost the whole menu. Fun, certainly. We enjoyed ourselves. The service is great. The room is lively and attractive, although the duodenal mirror-sculpture thing on the ceiling really had to go. But when I'm out with friends, I want to eat and talk and get full and taste stuff. Perhaps West is too subtle for me. And I'm guessing that, after dropping five or six hundred dollars for a party of four, a lot of people will have found the West experience too subtle. Unless, that is, they derived significant value from the fact of their presence at the epicenter of Vancouver culinary fashion, and the momentary convergence of their own behavior with that of Vancouver's food critics.

The best Fashion Food going. I believe it was. But then maybe that's all that has to be said about Fashion Food right there. Critics liked West because it was fashionable and if Geraghty had hung in there critics might still be liking him. He was, in any case, for that moment the chef in whose eyes they derived the Rousseauian sentiment of their existence. And if you think that's overdramatic, read this one bad review that West received, and you'll see that yearning etched in its every hysterical line.

"...find a new butter supplier and pile it on. Stick to your original version of frog's legs coddled in rich cream (whoever told you to go with a vinaigrette was mad or anorexic). Bring back the foie gras.

Give us sweetbreads and calf's liver.

Stop pulling your punches.

Show us something new and exciting.

Right now you look like a French chef in North American drag."

Those paragraph breaks were in the original too. Can you just see the reviewer's finger falling onto Geraghty's chest? Poke, poke, poke. *Give me what I want. Give it to me now.*

And then, a pleading tone creeps in.

"I know that's not you, Mr. Geraghty.

So why don't you step up to the plate and show us something this city has never seen before."

I hear: *Warren, Warren. We're lost without you!*

And we were shortly to lose him, too. He left Vancouver to cook at The Olde Bell in the Berkshire hamlet of Hurley. No more oompa-loompas. No more tweezers. No more shrieking, indignant critics, I suspect. Plaice with lemon and brown butter instead. Roast chicken dinner with scalloped potatoes. It's as if the reviewer above perhaps didn't know chef Geraghty terribly well, what he might actually like to cook, where he might choose to escape from the hectoring.

It's as if perhaps they weren't writing about him, his restaurant, or his food at all.

10

MY FRIEND WITH whom I shared that meal at long-ago Fuel in Kitsilano wrote a paper a couple of years ago called "Mandeville, Rousseau and the Political Economy of Fantasy." In it, he described the so-called Luxury Debates of the eighteenth century, in which people argued about the significance (good or bad) of a brand-new phenomenon in Atlantic-rim Europe at the time: the massive increase in the consumption of non-essentials, new clothes, new foods, new everything. It was a hot topic. And all the leading thinkers of the moment weighed in: Voltaire, Diderot, Montesquieu, Hutcheson, Hume, Adam Smith and others.

But the heart of the debate can be found in the disagreement between Mandeville and Rousseau.

Mandeville's position was influential and simple: Conspicuous luxury gave rise to envy, which provoked people into emulating each other, which made necessary the buying of things, which stimulated the economy, which ultimately was a tide that raised all boats. Rousseau agreed that envy and vanity were driving forces in consumer economies, but he thought that people were losing themselves in the process, surrendering their very identities to the whims of fashion. "We now seek our happiness in the opinion of others," wrote Mandeville, and Rousseau agreed. But unlike Mandeville, he thought it was a terrible development.

That's fashion, right there. Clothes fashion. Music fashion. Food fashion. Forget objective qualities (the very best pinot noir, ever). Forget subjective tastes (the perfect foie-gras preparation for my palate). Forget the very idea of anything being good or bad in the kitchen or on the table. Fashion doesn't believe in good or bad. It doesn't believe in anything. Fashion is endlessly relative, a moving target. Fashion is a chancer. It's all about reflected esteem, which is to say, the opinion of others. You'll know you're in a Food Fashion restaurant when you examine what's great about the experience—really, truly—and find that the best thing about it is the possibility of being seen there, a place that is momentarily the right place to be. I'm sorry we lost food to the Fashion Food Era, and that's really what I should have told the man at that long-ago literary festival.

I liked Fuel a lot, for what it's worth. I responded to that whole flavor-forward meat-centric thing that started happening in the mid-2000s. Of course, we didn't invent the trend. In London, a couple of years ahead of the trend here, you could hardly walk into a restaurant without meeting a pig's knuckle. I might not have gotten much real, visceral, tasting pleasure out of West, or Lumière before it, or Diva before that. But I knew how to enjoy Fuel's lamb-shoulder sandwich.

You just ate the thing. Talked to your companion and pretended there wasn't a food critic in the world, not me, not any of the ones quoted above. Nobody except perhaps James Barber, whose 14 syllables may be muttered under the breath from time to time, an incantation to be invoked after catching your reflection in any restaurant mirror.

"It's simple and delicious. So quit being such a snob."

11

I FELL FOR A girl over a meal in the Top of the Horizon once, the restaurant on the thirty-first floor of the Blue Horizon Hotel in downtown Vancouver. I was five years old, maybe six. Some Danish friends of my father's were in town and they had a daughter around my age. Her name may have been Bridget, or Heidi, I don't remember. She was this perfect doll: straw blond, green eyes. I remember she wore a white dress with a red ribbon around her waist. The adults put us across from one another at the end of the table, so it was like we had our own little dinner date going on by the window, sipping Shirley Temples and eating those 1970s shish kebabs of skewered cubes of meat and green peppers.

The food probably wasn't great. But the dining *experience* was seminal, because I think even at that age I sensed what magical things were possible with the right person and the right meal. The right view. The right rays of orange sunlight sloping off the shoulder of Stanley Park. When that little girl caught me gazing at her, she smiled back sweetly as if she'd been thinking exactly the same thing. And at the end of the evening, she gave me a blue-lacquered wooden horse that she'd brought all the way from Copenhagen.

Fast forward twenty-odd years. I was newly married, and had just taken a job with the Toronto Dominion Bank in Vancouver. My wife and I had moved from Toronto, but in the weeks before we finalized our apartment, the bank put us up at… the Blue Horizon Hotel. We didn't eat at the restaurant. These were our La Bodega years, and I'm not even sure Top of the Horizon was open at that time. But while unpacking, we came across an old scrapbook my wife had kept as a girl. And tucked into its pages was a photo of her when she was five. I hadn't seen the picture before or any other one of her at that age. Which allowed me to discover—in a strange temporal rush, that feeling of a vortex opening and connecting you to a very particular moment and set of feelings from the past—just how firmly that long-ago meal had stayed in my subconscious. How seamlessly woven into memory it had been. Because looking at that picture of my wife, I realized that at five years of age, and right at the same time, she and Bridget/Heidi had looked exactly alike.

12

––––––– // –––––––

SEMINAL MEALS, FORMATIVE meals. The plates and flavors we never forget.

I've been poring over old menus and recipe cards from the mid-seventies, trying to push myself back in time. It's one thing to understand how our long-ago evangelists changed the food world in unexpected, even unpredictable ways. But can we the diners and review readers push ourselves back? Can we ever really understand what came before, what food was like before the revolution hit, before we surrendered it to the tossing of fashion's seas?

I suppose I'm the kind of food lover who would try. I have an obvious fondness for the old school. My heroes Barber and Pépin are guys who both published recipes for a stuffed whole head of cabbage. (You don't see that on many menus, these days.) I always appreciated how settled they both seemed to be in their own culinary practices. Not much would change about either of them from the beginning to the end of their public cooking careers.

In Pépin's case, that single-mindedness made for some early television comedy. Here's a guy who'd been working in the near-military environs of European kitchens since the age of twelve, trying to be all casual and easygoing and ready for prime time. (Pépin aired on PBS, but food television more broadly has now evolved to the point that he would be terminally out of place—but more on that later.) For a while there Pépin did try—or PBS tried—and so we had him cooking with his daughter,

Claudine, visibly resisting the impulse to snatch the kitchen tools away from her every time she cut up an onion or peeled a carrot the wrong way.

Of course fashion lives in the contrast to this idea of right or wrong ways. So, after the revolution, one of the most obvious things we've probably all noticed is that there are only better and better ways to do things, there is only the endless pursuit of the best in any given category. You know people like this: who only buy a particular kind of olive oil or *fleur de sel*, or who will only drink coffee made by a Clover espresso machine. It is worth remembering how this was, very briefly, tamped down in the wake of the 2008/2009 global financial turmoil. Vancouver had a slowdown, but like real estate prices in this part of the world, the foodie world has stormed back, proving that consumers do not *unlearn* what they've been taught by one another. We do not stop wanting new bold flavors, innovative techniques, farm-to-table virtuosity, or any of the other values that we adopted post-frozen-mixed-veg.

I found myself thinking about that last point during a recent visit with some friends who have a daughter the same age as our son (five years old, echoes of the Top of the Horizon). We adults were sitting around on the deck, and we overheard the two of them down at the bottom of the garden. What were they talking about? Not *Monsters vs Aliens* or the meanest kid in their class. They were talking about food. Specifically, we tuned in just in time to hear the little girl ask my son if he liked quail. My son said he wasn't sure as he'd never tried it, but did she like truffles?

My son has tried truffles *once*, I stress. A couple of drops of infused oil on his scrambled eggs. I do recall the look on his face while he chewed, however. His eyes went all trippy and drifted past the horizon, as if he had found some great answer floating there, visible to anyone who could see into a fifth dimension. Then he swallowed and refocused on his toast, eating it bite by bite until it was gone. Then he did this thing he does at moments of pinnacle culinary pleasure, which I did not teach him. I don't know where he got this one, probably daycare. He raised his arms, clapped both his hands over his head, and yelled: "Yummy!"

Fine. Yummy. I happen to agree. But what I found interesting, watching the two kids together, is how they enacted the exact underlying process that drives the upward spiral of refinement and good taste in the rest of us. They were competing. She put an idea on the table: eating quail, and the sophistication and maturity that this conferred on the five-year-old in question. My son picked up the idea, even though I'm quite confident that he was thinking about something else entirely up to that moment (*Monsters vs. Aliens* quite likely). There they were, gripped by the same desire, vying for the prize of top-dog connoisseur. For a few seconds, anyway. And then, because they're kids, they went off to play and forgot all about it while the adults laughed behind their hands and rolled their eyes and were secretly a little proud to have raised kids with tastes *just like their own.*

In a world of fashion we copy ideas from one another: we pick things up and drop them, we vie with each other for esteem, we compete and imitate. But, at least with food, and at least among five-year-olds, it was not always thus. And I feel confident saying this because I just know that even if Bridget/Heidi had spoken English, we would not have known to think it a cool idea to spend the evening talking about whether I liked pickled herring and she ate homemade granola.

And, of course, I take responsibility for my role in my son's development. I talk food at home, and I've become a food writer myself over the years. One recent piece had me single-hand-edly preparing menus from the fanatical recipes of chefs Daniel Humm, Heston Blumenthal, René Redzepi and Thomas Keller. Fanatical how? Fanatical like a recipe for roast turbot with eighty-four ingredients. Like preparations calling for xanthan gum and agar agar, nitrogen and transglutaminase (which I had to have shipped to me FedEx from a chef in Alabama). Fanatical like instructions to use twenty small *muikku* (a small freshwater whitefish) or to sous-vide five different components of a dish over fifteen hours. These are preparations that depend on a full *brigade de cuisine* and commercial-grade pantries and kitchens.

My son watched me tackle these alone in our small home kitchen over the two and a half weeks it took me to prepare four meals. He schmecked his way through a bowl of langoustine in celery cream and green apple snow. He ate the edible dirt in which Redzepi's "vegetable field" is planted. Onions with blue-berry and spruce shoots. Brined and sous-vided pork belly with chard and champagne vinaigrette. He noshed on halibut with pickled daikon, daikon vinaigrette, citrus beurre blanc and a gar-nish of edamame and citrus candy. He's still asking me for "that fish you made," a preparation I'm unlikely to repeat until the next time I have *three days to prepare dinner*. But it's inevitable in this process that he would come to assume merely by watching me and eating what's put in front of him that food is a topic on which one is supposed to opine.

"Do you like quail?"

"I'm not sure. Do you like truffles? Yummy!"

Ask my kid about Rule Number One. Maybe I got this wrong, because he won't say: *Don't steal*, or *Make sure you graduate from medical school*. Instead, because I obviously once said some-thing to make him think this is the cardinal rule of existence, he'll say: *Never, ever, eat at McDonald's*.

I had to break it to him eventually. I have, in the past, eaten at McDonald's, although only under one strict set of conditions: when embarking early on a road trip. So I've actually eaten quite a few Egg McMuffins behind the wheel. And while they are truly awful on just about every level, they're perfect too, because every Egg McMuffin I've ever had has been exactly like the first one I had. Here's a product that competes with nothing, which is beyond fashion. And that still seems in a way virtuous to me.

We went driving early one Saturday morning, just my son and I. He piped up from the back seat: "Is this a road trip?" I knew where that question was heading. And so we invoked the Limitations and Exceptions sub-clause of Rule Number One together and hit the nearest drive-through. He took about a minute to scarf down an Egg McMuffin and one of those potato-confit shingles they call hash browns.

Then he told me he felt sick.

13

//

MAINTAIN SOME OF the old family recipes in my own kitchen today. When I went away to school for the first time, I carried away a clutch of recipe cards, now brown with age and stained with use. The cuisine to which they bear witness is a strange hybrid one, the result of my strange hybrid background. My mother was a German Jewish refugee after the war, whose family ended up settling in Ecuador. My Canadian father was a

nomad by personal choice, living in the Philippines and traveling through Hong Kong, South East Asia, Europe and the U.S.
before taking a job in South America, where he met my mother.
They ended up staying there and having five kids before return-
ing to Canada to settle in West Vancouver. And so, by the time
I was first forming memories of food, that was the pastiche of
personalities and experiences and places and traditions that
informed our cuisine.

We ate my mother's truncated childhood: spaetzle, rouladen,
long-simmered pot roasts, buttered carrots, and cookies made
with ground almonds and hazelnuts and dusted with icing
sugar. We also ate the memories my father had of the long-ago
road: pomegranates and plantains, yams, chili peppers, egg-
plant, mangoes, the occasional wheel of brie. And when it came
time for me to go away to university, I remember sitting with
my mother at the kitchen table and going through her recipe
box and copying out my favorites. I've lost most of those cards.
But the ones that remain read like a *menu fixe* at a very unusual
restaurant that only my family could run, and at which perhaps
only my family would ever dine.

Lentil soup, Brazilian rice, the aforementioned ceviche and
arroz con pollo, plus two different recipes for beef stroganoff, one
of which is actually made with hamburger.

That last item there sounds pretty dreadful, I realize. But
it introduces an important point about the comfort of family recipes, even when the expertise and refinement you have
acquired makes you well aware that a given dish could be
greatly improved. Hamburger stroganoff, for example. On
paper, this is a recipe that could use much refinement. It calls for
Worcestershire sauce and soy sauce, one can of mushrooms and
another of cream of chicken soup. Every time I make this dish—
say, once every five years—I think of how it could be improved,

how really, it *demands* to be improved.

Then I just head on down to the grocery store and get the cream of chicken soup and make it the old-school way. And the stuff is good. In fact, it kicks your ass in a very particular way. It says to you: What? *You were planning to refine your own memories?*

At a chef friend's house the other day, discussing this very topic, I noticed that he kept French's mustard in the fridge. I pulled it out, held it up. I said: "Are you serious here? You're like one of the best cooks I've ever met in my life and you're using French's mustard?" He shrugged and grinned. It goes into the batter of a particular fried-fish recipe that he learned from a very old friend whose family owns a restaurant in Baja. It's in the warp and woof of the dish. It can't be changed without unraveling the whole thing. So when it's time to make that dish, he digs out the French's mustard. Don't even talk to him about whether Dijon would be better because of course it *wouldn't be.*

I have a French's mustard confession. If you're squeamish, this next paragraph may not be for you. I cook this dish reasonably often at home, but never for friends. I just don't think they're up for it and I'd like them to stay friends. It's one of my mother's all-time classics: beef tongue in mustard sauce. Say it in French if you have to—it definitely sounds better: *langue de boeuf á la moutarde.* Here's how you do it, for those of you who like the nasty bits:

Simmer a beef tongue in water with carrots, onions, celery, peppercorns and garlic cloves. When the tongue is fork-tender— about three hours for a 3- to 4-pound tongue—remove it from the liquid and skin it. Next, make yourself a white sauce using butter and flour and the simmering liquid. Finally, the crucial step here... dig out the French's mustard from the back of the fridge and use a couple of tablespoons to turn your white sauce brilliantly (almost blindingly) yellow. Adjust seasonings. Serve over rice with green beans.

Why not go with Dijon mustard here? See above. Because it wouldn't be better. Which is the same reason, incidentally, I sometimes horrify my wife by serving this dish with canned green beans. Yeah I know. But a can of green beans flown in from Chile lends the meal a 1970s super-authenticity that it would otherwise lack. It gives the meal stability, a rootedness in the pre-fashion era. The plate aspiring to be nothing more than what it has always been.

And it's not just comforting, either. It tastes fantastic too.

14

―――――//―――――

I WANT TO MAKE a case for the past, for history. Not that we should return to it, but that we might do well to understand it better. Take the farm-to-table category. It can't even really be referred to as a phenomenon anymore, because in the past twelve years or so it's grown from a flaky niche into one of the foundational values in restaurant cuisine. A quick Google search in Vancouver and I can pull up multiple "10 Best Farm to Table" lists, like those published by Yelp or Gadling Travel, and find almost no overlap. Over at Urbanspoon, on their page "Vancouver Farm to Table Restaurants," you can choose from over sixty entries.

Clearly, at that level of penetration the advantages in using the label overwhelm the possibility of proving it means anything in reality. Is that falafel shop on Commercial drive really "farm to table"? Is it even possible to make a farm to table falafel in Vancouver?

But the answer doesn't matter anyway. The bigger point is that farm to table is an almost perfectly inverted claim to that made on menus in Vancouver other cities in the sixties and seventies, where establishments strained to make clear that they knew which place on earth to find the best version of any ingredient. I have a few dozen old menus open on the desk in front of me here. And in these restaurants a sole is always from Dover, a crab is always Alaska King, a chateaubriand is always going to be served with sauce Béarnaise from France, and rice will never be anything other than wild and from Manitoba. Not a Saskatchewan chickpea in sight.

In the pre-globalization era, in other words, while it meant something to fly to Paris, it also meant a lot to fly Paris over here: the ingredients, the menu, the whole repertoire of sauces. Which is more or less what was going on in the dining rooms at Chez Joel and Le Napoléon and L'Escargot—three Vancouver restaurants that had almost identical menus, from the *escargot de Bourgogne* to the *ris de veau à la crème*. Those restaurateurs and diners were just reaching out for what was considered to be the best.

Think, then, how confusing it would have been to ask a fine diner of that era to cultivate an interest in Skeena steelhead instead, or Salt Spring Island lamb, or beef from Pemberton. We tend to accept that such a request would have been ludicrous, but for the wrong reasons. We think: Well, of course a 1970s diner could not appreciate local food as we do, because we have educated ourselves over the intervening years. We have voyaged into the future—in years and sophistication—and left those proto-foodies of yesteryear behind.

But I don't think that's the reason why the request would be ludicrous. The *locavore* ethic of today would not have seemed to those diners like idea from the future, but a throwback to the past. An erecting of walls around the encampment of Vancouver. A re-embrace of medieval insularity and ignorance. Perhaps even a conservative bigotry from which mid-seventies liberals thought they had only just recently been freed.

We know that new information has since been brought to the table. In understanding our world to be interconnected—culturally, environmentally—it's now high boorishness, a kind of anti-human insensitivity, to expect the world to ship its delicacies to the highest bidder in foreign lands. So the farmers' markets are jammed with people carrying $40 bags of heirloom tomatoes. So the waiter at the Pointe Restaurant in the Wick-aninnish Inn can offer a jug of water to the table, uttering the words in a tremulous whisper: "Local water?" And so, in Ganges the other summer, I could witness an American tourist planning a barbecue wave aside the organic chickens on offer because they weren't from the island.

"Where are they from?" I asked the woman, who stood staring after the man, red-faced with exasperation.

"Duncan," she said. "That's like what, ten kilometers away?"

That sea change in tastes—from foreign exotic to local authentic—may well be a net gain in the sense that it has made people take food more seriously, thereby decreasing the likelihood that they will eat factory-processed crap from, say, McDonald's. Only it remains a profound irony to me that foodies of our era will not give the seventies ethos any credit for having made the culinary eureka-moments of our present day possible. After all, were it not for the exploratory, outward-looking zeal of our foodie ancestors, how would our awareness of the globe's interconnectivity ever have arisen, such that we might draw back from it, scared at what we have wrought? Just what kind of person was eating jellied madrilène Orloff at the Carriage Room in the late sixties and early seventies, if not someone who sensed themselves complexly linked to distant traditions? Because that's the ancestor of our present-day agrimoral fixations right there, folks: consommé with tomatoes and chives served cold and a bit of veal Orloff aspic'd into the bottom of the bowl.

But no, we don't give the past much credit because we believe ourselves to be smarter than our forebears. Or, in the riptides of a fashion-obsessed world, smarter even than the dummies who were high on the radar last month, or last week. This constant toppling and overturning, this relentless

high-contact game of usurpation. Check out the big food stars
of our era and recall that the foodie sensibility of an earlier generation was captured by the genteel enthusiasms of Elizabeth
David and M.K. Fisher. Now you have the bellowing bro-itude
of Guy Fieri stuffing sandwiches into his face, or the ridiculous
pontification of Alton Brown on the future of recipe-writing
(Google up that video for a head-scratching yawn). Paula Deen
counseling kids to eat cheesecake for breakfast. Andrew Zimmern eating a mosquito egg or an octopus bile sac or a bull
rectum. Zimmern could put literally *anything* into his mouth
and it wouldn't make any difference. Dried yak turds. Why not?
It's *bizarre*, people.

And it reflects a growing, gnawing insatiability at the heart
of these affairs. It's been a number of years since it was published, but the book *The Man Who Ate the World*, by U.K. food
critic Jay Rayner, is without a doubt the charter document of
this nation of anxious foodies. Here you have a man on a world
tour of the fanciest restaurants, staggering through galaxies of
Michelin stars, at the nauseating end of which Rayner's central
point is that he remains as hungry and irritable as ever. Overfed
and underfed. Stuffed and miserable.

Where did all this come from in food? What the hell is
everybody looking for? Of course, as it must be in all realms
governed by fashion, the answer is everything and nothing.
What's good and truly satisfying in the Food Fashion Era is an
endlessly moving target. Fieri will never find a taco not worth
a fist bump and a "Shut the front DOOR!" Brown will forever
wax philosophically on topics not needing it, Deen has diabe-
tes, Zimmern is eating yak turds as we speak. And Rayner is
still hungry, still roving the world's dining rooms in search of a
perfect meal he doesn't want to find because that would mean
nobody would need him anymore.

15

————————— // —————————

I WANTED TO TRY the impossible, to punch back through time. What was it like to eat before the revolution? Could I get back to that mindset? I mentioned this to a food critic I know and she frowned and said, "Well, like *what* for example will you cook?"

I had only picked one dish at that point, from this stack of 1970s menus. So I told them, "Prawns in Canadian Club sauce, an appetizer from the Quarry House in Queen Elizabeth Park, 1977."

She took a step back, hand to her throat, and said, "Eeew."

Well, exactly so. What could be more disgustingly out of touch than prawns cooked in Canadian Club rye whiskey? How dreadfully embarrassing. What if someone were to actually see me eating it?

I needed backup, so I convinced a friend to host the party and help me cook. If there were such a thing as a celebrity home cook—that is, a cook with a fan base but no restaurant or television show—I'm fairly sure this friend would qualify. So prolific a host is he that, on more than one occasion, having enjoyed a late dinner at his house, I've called the next morning to say thanks and found him in the midst of hosting a brunch.

We got together at a café on West Broadway to look at a stack of menus I had gathered from the Vancouver Archives and from the personal menu collection of the very helpful Joan

Cross, wife of legendary local food and wine critic Sid Cross, with whom she has sampled Vancouver restaurants for the better part of four decades.

My friend and I spent the morning traveling back in time. As you might expect, some of the mid-seventies dishes did look terminally dated. Turtle soup, for example, is unlikely to hit menus again soon, given that it involves eating an endangered species. I remember ordering it once myself at a Cajun place downtown (remember Cajun places?). It was strangely delicious, velvety and tangy at once, though I do remember being vaguely unsettled by an ovoid bone I found floating in it.

Other presentations seemed somehow to have passed out of aesthetic reach. I wanted to like them but could come to no other conclusion than that they would be disgusting. I cite the Vancouver Fizz, which Il Giardino used to serve in the early eighties: vodka, triple sec, Kahlua, orange juice and whipping cream—a boozy Orange Julius as best I can make out, without any fizz. Ditto the Carpetbagger Steak, which they used to serve at the old Timber Club. What you do here is take oysters and mushrooms and sauté them in butter, then stir in crumbled bacon, blue cheese, parsley and Sauternes (cough). Then you stuff all that into a pocket in the side of a piece of beef filet and cook to the desired degree of done-ness. It's not the unfashionability of this dish that disturbs me. It's the idea of that gray mass in the middle of my steak.

But quite a lot of what we found in those menus seemed both do-able and delicious. And it was interesting to see the cultural influences that ran through haute cuisine back then. Northern Europe was the last exotic place many people had been, in those post-war decades. And you read this in these menus. You could get stroganoff all over town, even in the fancy places. Top of the Horizon had it. So did the Carriage Room and the William Tell. Schnitzel, too, which was dressed up very finely indeed at the Quarry House, with asparagus and crab legs and an anointing of sauce Béarnaise.

If there was any Asian influence in evidence at the high end, it tended more toward Bali Hai than Beijing. This was the heyday of Trader Vic's. Lots of places snuck in a tropical note, as if to provide for the member of the party who was planning to get a little tipsy and loud. For the Jackie Gleason on hand, there would be the Seafood Waikiki at the Devonshire Seafood House, baked in a papaya with a light curry sauce. (That one actually doesn't sound so great to me—something about hot papaya.) But I'm prepared to bet that the Bongo Bongo soup at Trader Vic's, creamed with spinach and oysters, tasted pretty decent with a shake of Tabasco and a rum drink on the side. Ditto the Salad of the Sea with prawns and crab on hearts of palm at the Cloud 9.

There were other dishes that recommended themselves for their ubiquity at the time. Things that flamed up big at the table were popular. Steak Diane and steak *au poivre* flambé could be found all over town. It makes you realize why restaurateurs all opened up their kitchens to the dining room in the eighties. Their cooks had spent the seventies trotting the kitchen out into the dining room with every second dish. Lobsters Thermidor and Newburg were also big. Things dressed up "Louis" or "Rockefeller," "Strasbourg" or "Jurassienne." Meat sauced with a ladle of Hollandaise or Béarnaise. And surely the *tournedos de boeuf* Rossini in Bordelaise sauce was the pinnacle expression of seventies super-fine, with its rich incorporation of filet mignon, foie gras, truffles, plus a sauce of port, brandy, Madeira and demi-glaze. Here's a dish to make contemporary foodies go "Eeew," but I dare any one of them to sit down in front of an appropriate portion, a nicely balanced proto-tower atop a crostini, and not eat the thing immediately.

In the end, though, we went with dishes that captured the essential paradoxes of the assignment. That is, dishes that were hugely popular but are nowhere to be found on cool menus today, and which don't sound exciting or interesting, but which—using good ingredients and maybe scaling portions back a bit—could actually look and taste great.

And here's where we ended up.

Menu Fixe

Special cocktail: the Nine O'Clock Gun

Local spot-prawn skewer with Canadian Club sauce

Duck *à l'orange* with braised endive and wild-rice pilaf

Steak Diane with asparagus Polonaise

and potatoes Parisienne

Peach Melba

Allowing for the fact that I'm reviewing myself, here's the verdict:

Awesome appetizer. I'd make this anytime. The local spot prawns were out of the water that afternoon, steamed live. And don't let a foodie dissuade you from making a sauce out of Canadian Club, either. We sleeked out the classic Scottish shellfish and whiskey recipe, using the Quarry House's rye idea and amping the seasonings. We also nixed the broiled-cheese stage that normally comes at the end of this preparation. And it was a hit: the sauce velvety, a touch of sweet and heat, a trace of thyme.

Duck *à l'orange*, meanwhile. Campy but great stuff. Do use Grand Marnier in the sauce, and maybe a bit in the chef. This is an old-fashioned dish and you want it sticky, baby. Put a tiny puddle down under the duck, which you can cook to the new-era rosy standard, and the sweet foils wonderfully against the caramelized duck skin. You do need some edge on this plate, and the tart endive gives it, cooked to brown and crispy at the edges. Steak Diane, likewise—much better than you might think. There are lots of ways to ruin this dish by overcooking or oversaucing it. But the cognac cream with the foresty back-flavor of the mushrooms is high-end comfort. And the geyser of flames convinces people you know what you're doing, even if you don't.

We did not make a special cocktail in the end. The Nine O'Clock Gun seemed to fit the twin paradox nicely: nowhere to be found today and, with rum and vermouth, not sounding particularly good either. But in the mad Saturday afternoon rush to provision our dinner for ten, the rum and vermouth never ended up on either of our shopping lists.

So we toasted each other with the dinner wine instead, picked as most suitable to the era: a non-intrusive, pre-fruit-bomb Rhône from Perrin et Fils. We toasted the moment and all the moments that led up to it. And we hoped for future moments quite the same.

To you and you and you and you. And to *you*, Bridget/Heidi, wherever you are.

EPILOGUE

FIVE YEARS AGO I went to Spain. I walked across it. An old college friend of mine talked me into it—over dinner. That's where these kinds of plans are inevitably hatched. He said to me: "I'm going to walk 800 kilometers on foot through Basque Country, Cantabria, Asturias and Galicia, and I'd like you to come." Which was crazy, clearly. But we'd just had an amazing meal—at Fergus Henderson's restaurant St. John in London, where I was fortunate to have been sent on assignment.

It was a good thing he asked me at the particular moment that he did. Had my friend asked me at another time, I might have had the time to think of an excuse not to do it. In St. John, with an earthy meal of roast bone marrow salad and tripe fritters so recently inside me, the idea of living life in an ultra-simplified way for a while—being a dharma bum for a month, basically—well, all this made a certain kind of sense, in the moment.

Which is how I ended up hoofing it from Irun, just west of the Pyrenees, all the way west along the famous old pilgrimage route to Santiago de Compostela.

Trips like these have many plot lines, of course. The physical challenge is one (blisters, hamstrings, et cetera). Coming to an understanding of why you're doing it in the first place is another (pilgrims like to talk on this topic, I discovered). And food, happily, was also a daily story. Where to eat? Is this a *tapas* or a *fabada* town? Do you think that tortilla has been sitting on the bar since this morning? And then, confessedly, this question from late in the trip: God, do you think we'll be able to find any decent Japanese food in Santiago?

Sacrilege, I know. Four weeks on the road can do strange things to you. I did actually reach a point where I didn't want to eat any more cured pork products. (I've since recovered.) But *before* that, we had many fine Spanish meals, including one very humble meal (eight euro, about twelve bucks) that stood out as something in the order of an epiphany.

Here's how that one happened. We'd pulled into

Markina-Xemein, deep in the green hills of the Biscay province of Basque country, east of Bilbao. The day had been longer than we'd expected, twenty-five kilometers on foot, up and down through forests and valleys, along laneways, through fields, across streams. Six hours of walking later, down along the sloping ridgeline above the town, knees screaming, missing a turn-off, doubling back, staggering into town under still-hot later afternoon sun.

Too tired, too disoriented to make sense of the map in the town square, we phoned the pension where we were booked and the woman who ran the place came and rescued us in her tiny car. We stank. We couldn't really communicate in Spanish, much less Basque. She only smiled and rolled the windows down, then drove us up the hill to the pension, but not before stopping and arranging for our dinner at a restaurant on the square. Good food, she gestured, speaking Basque but making her point. Good, hot food. You can go there later. They're expecting you.

We crashed. Woke an hour later, starving. So it was on this early evening in July that we found ourselves in the Markina-Xemein town square, at a corner table in a restaurant considered to be the best. We looked around, assessing. It was an interesting room, obviously once quite grand. The room was wide, with high ceilings, ornate light fixtures. The chairs were formal high-backed jobs, set up around large square dining tables. The room had once been a place where people came to step out, to be *seen*. But it was equally clear that all that had changed, and a long time ago. The place was dusty, probably could have used a cleaning. The formal dining tables were now clothed in paper. And judging from the people there, the room had aged and mellowed from a fashionable scene into a something more like a community living room. There were city workers in orange neon vests eating grilled fish across the way. Guys in rumpled suits stretching out after-work brandies with snack-style *pintxos*: olives on skewers, anchovies and bread. A couple of young women in colorful cycling gear tucking into a mid-ride snack of *salad mixta*. (Spain must surely consume more iceberg lettuce and canned tuna than any other nation on earth.)

When it came time for us to order, we chose from a typical daily menu: a few options each for a starter, a main, a dessert and a choice of wine or beer. The woman working the front gave us our choices in Spanish, rightly assuming we wouldn't understand a word of Basque. So we had to pick out the six or eight words of Spanish we recognized and order accordingly. My friend went for the *macaroni*. ("Con queso?" he asked. "Con tomate," she answered. "Like Chef Boyardee," I said to him in English.)

For me: *patatas con chorizo*. And I still remember distinctly what I *thought* I was going to get. I had a picture from Epicurious or maybe Saveur in my head: crisp, golden, pan fried potatoes tossed with chunks of sautéed chorizo, a bit of parsley on top. Maybe a basket of bread on the side. But what arrived in fact (and in scant minutes) was a large tureen of boiled potatoes, cooked soft and served steaming in their cooking liquid. No evidence of chorizo but for the residual color of the famous sausage, which stained the entire dish a brilliant orange.

I was disappointed, I'll admit. In fact, I took a picture of the dish with my phone, thinking that I'd use it at some later point to remind myself ironically of what had come out of the kitchen to greet my uptown, auto-gastronomic expectations. But then I tried it. And it tasted fantastic. Rich with chorizo flavor, even if there was only a single nub of the stuff at the bottom of the tureen. Simple fare. Exactly the kind of thing you wanted to eat after a day spent climbing the Basque hills. And getting somewhere beyond its own flavor in the delivery, somehow. Filling, yes. But also *satisfying*. A meal that left me completed for the moment, in search of nothing further. Sure I'd be ravenous again after the next twenty-five kilometers, after the next dozen ridgelines had been crossed. But those laneways and forests and fields and valleys and challenges and conflicts all lay in the future. I was only in that moment and utterly satisfied, desiring nothing. And I felt great. A pinnacle, summit feeling. It wasn't just a matter of having accidentally ordered the best thing off the menu, of having been expectant, then dubious, and then impossibly surprised. It was a matter of having ordered the best thing off of any menu anywhere in the world at just that moment.

The world continued to turn. The walk went on. Valleys and hilltops. There were steep ridges before Pola de Allande and Grandas de Salime, where the white wind turbines rotated in the rushing air.

And we fed stupendously.

Slow-roasted lamb shoulders, platters of octopus and smoked ham, oxtails, *bocadillos* with thick slices of cheese or rings of fried calamari. In Castro-Urdiales, eaten while looking out over boats in the harbor, a whole monkfish cooked in oil with garlic. In El Haya, a slab of beef *churleton* between us, grilled an inch and a half thick and served with *pimiento piquillo*. And all of that was then just as you would find it now, quite unchanged were you to walk that route today or tomorrow or in ten years time, I'm confident. At the roadside café just past Berducedo, look for the wasp's nest in the bathroom and the red chickens out front running riot between the legs of the table where the owner has laid out a plate of hazelnuts for pilgrims, a small hammer provided for cracking.

The world continued to turn here too, but with no such inclination or capacity for stasis. From that flourishing of early nineties evangelism, you could say, flowed directly that gushing review of Diva, from which flowed in turn the long daisy chain of chefs and rooms and Food Network shows that have followed. At the moment of writing, embedded as I am now myself in that market of food opinion, I see the consumerist West teeming with food talk—a million Food Network viewers a night, 150 million Yelp and Urbanspoon visits monthly—a discussion so massively parallel it's almost miraculous to think that the phenomenon traces its roots to seminal cook/critics like Barber, like Childs. Like Mike Kalina, who seemed to mark the shift of food epochs with his passing.

Kalina as sacrificial victim. Food as religious ritual. I'm pushing it, but barely. Consumerism as article of faith is an old idea. It's been fifteen years since the ad men at Young & Rubicam wrote in a *Financial Times* editorial: "Brands are the new religion. People turn to them for meaning." And food, in this respect—restaurants, ingredients, cooking supplies, kitchens, cookbooks—is a consumer realm like any other. Insofar as it is providing people with a sense of meaning, it will have its anointed saints, blessed sacraments, and ignoble paragons of sin.

My family broke bread and took wine at The Farmer's Apprentice this past week. For the purposes of this story, chef David Gunawan's newest Vancouver restaurant can be considered the point furthest down the river. It's as far as we've journeyed together. It's where the flow of appetite and enthusiasm and mimetic desire have taken us: a gastronomic forty-seater on West Seventh in Kitsilano, just off what used to be gallery row—before all the galleries vacated for the Terminal Street flats where the rents are cheaper.

It is useful to glance over your shoulder when sitting down to dine at an establishment like The Farmers Apprentice, to assess if only briefly how we arrived in this room. Sophistication thirty years ago—as can be read clearly on those old menus I used for my retro-dinner party—can be traced to three core values. The first is the faithful reproduction of classical continental preparations within a relatively few north European and Italian traditions. For the first dozen years of the Vancouver Restaurant Awards, the prize went eleven times to a restaurant working explicitly in a continental tradition. The second value is the elegance, which is to say relatively muted flavor profiles of those cuisines. (I couldn't resist this impulse myself, intensifying that classic whiskey sauce with shallots, cayenne and fresh thyme before thickening with whole grain mustard and heavy cream.) The third of these three values was the proud international sourcing of ingredients, a gesture to show sophistication by using the best in the world.

It's almost obvious, in retrospect, how these values would evolve by reaction. Sophistication in dining today is the precise and predictable inversion of what came before. From the rigidity of those continental traditions has come the flourishing of gastronomic innovation: new equipment, new techniques, new dishes entirely. From the restrained elegance of those flavorings has come the bold expansion of seasonings and unexpected flavor pairings. And from the impulse to source internationally, to celebrate the exotic, has come a sudden and intense attention paid to the simplicity and relative informality of the local.

Different chefs clearly weight these values differently. But in Vancouver and urban zones across the West today, you'll be hard-pressed to find a high-end restaurant that isn't explicitly shaped around some combination of these ideas: inventive, flavor-forward dishes, with an emphasis on local ingredients. It was only appropriate then that on the twenty-fifth anniversary of the Vancouver Restaurant Awards, The Farmer's Apprentice should win highest honors. Best Restaurant of the Year. Best New Restaurant of the Year. Best Casual Restaurant of the Year. It really is the restaurant toward which we've been heading for a long time.

And it is, without a doubt, an intense and surprising and local experience. A curious room: equal parts hole-in-the-wall comfort station and mad scientist's lair. There are simple wood tables, jars of pickles on shelves, a warm lit sidebar with a turntable and a stack of vinyl from which diners are encouraged to choose. But then there's the kitchen, which is so open that you feel like you're eating in it, and which pulses with chaotic culinary energy as Gunawan and his cooks and dishwashers square-dance around the Rational oven and the Kamado grill and a single prep table stacked with what would appear to be 800 plastic tubs of mis en place.

Egg yolk, potato foam, onion, granola.

Octopus, salsa verde, fennel, potato, salmon roe.

Chicken liver and foie gras parfait, winter vegetables in textures.

Those are the menu listings, by the way, not my description of them. Yes, The Farmer's Apprentice adheres to that slightly annoying trend to list only ingredients, not preparations. But that is no doubt part of the impulse to surprise. Who puts an egg yolk on granola and why? You have to order the dish to find out. And when you do, it arrives at your table on seventies-evocative pottery, tabled by one of the cooks trotting out from the kitchen in stained whites, presenting like a kind of gastronomically geeked-out comfort fare. Of course it's all farm to table, as the name suggests. Gunawan reveres farmers of heritage breeds and seeds. But that earthy sensibility is always refracted through layers of technique and flavor combinations that, let's just be honest, nobody would think of as comforting.

Olives smoked for four hours. Oysters sous vided forty minutes and topped with green radish, grapefruit granite and a splash of sake kasu cream. Do these things taste good? Those two certainly did and ditto the onion butter, which I would eat every day if I could. Even the stranger dishes succeed by being intense, intricate, inventive. That octopus was fork tender with traces of grill smoke, tasting strongly of the sea; though it really came to life only when every component of the dish was precariously combined into a single bite (a potato chip with a bead of salmon roe, a sliver of fennel). And that curious granola dish. Swirled together with the yolk and potato foam and caramelized shallots, you get a creamy, rich and delicious porridge that you couldn't have anticipated enjoying and can't quite believe you did afterward, either. We scraped the bowl and found ourselves pleasantly perplexed.

There were a couple of misfires. Inventive, bold and local dishes that left me wondering if they needed to be invented. The liver foie gras parfait didn't work, something about the mouth-feel of foamed offal. The risotto was a brilliant Melmac green and perfectly cooked, but the sea cucumber didn't add much beyond being a weird protein you probably haven't tried before.

In the end—after we'd prodded and poked and tasted the dishes, and wrinkled our brows and talked about each one like it was a science experiment—we had to agree that The Farmer's Apprentice was a success on Gunawan's own terms. This is a chef who told his riveted Pecha Kucha crowd: "We don't want you to like everything about us. It's boring to love everything. I'd rather you like one dish and hate another and find two OK, then have a dessert that's amazing!"

Gunawan got nervous laughs saying that in 2014. One imagines him being run out of town in 1984.

After paying the bill at The Farmer's Apprentice, my wife and son and I did something we rarely do: we lingered and continued to talk about what we'd just eaten. It wasn't because we thought we were supposed to or because it was so expensive we were trying to justify the meal post-purchase. The food really was, in its enshrinement of those three contemporary values, sufficiently interesting to bear discussion.

"I liked the onion butter," my son said. "And the olives. And the porridge with the egg."

We all agreed on those, although my wife and I were split on the octopus.

"I don't think that was really a salsa verde," I said. "More like a chimichurri."

Then my son said: "What's the best thing you ever ate, ever."

So we thought about that for a while. My wife remembered a dish of Jacques Pépin's I used to cook back in the day when I was working my way through La Technique and La Methode. A real labour of love, this one. It involved gutting and cleaning squid, then stuffing them with a forcemeat made of their tentacles chopped and sautéed with shallots, garlic, mushrooms, breadcrumbs. Seasoned only with salt and pepper, the dish was finished quickly in the oven with a sauce of diced tomatoes, saffron and white wine.

"Why don't you make that anymore?" she wondered aloud.

But we both knew why. Because we'd been eating a lot of tacos at our house lately. Pressure cooker carnitas made with achiote and pasilla, from a technique I came across in Modernist Cuisine Volume 3: Animals and Plants. Innovation, bold flavors, Berkshire pork from up the valley.

My son was still looking at me, waiting for my answer. I

pulled out my phone and paged through the pictures. I had to page back a long way—there had been a lot of meals between The Farmers Apprentice and that long-ago moment. Then I found it. Brilliant orange. Blue and white tureen, cracked around the rim. Paper tablecloth.

I showed him. He said: "What is it?"

I told him the short version. *Patatas con chorizo*. Markina-Xemein . End of a very, very long day.

My son was squinting. "Um... Was it good?"

So I was able to answer the question, finally. The whole truth. "It was the best, ever."

Photo by Dave Middleton

ABOUT THE AUTHOR

Timothy Taylor is an award winning author
and journalist. He has published two works of
nonfiction and four works of fiction, including
The Blue Light Project and Stanley Park. He
lives in Vancouver, BC.

Made in the USA
San Bernardino, CA
03 July 2014